W9-AXQ-567

The Missing Nose Flute
and Other Mysteries of Life

Nick Bantock

▪▪▪▪▪▪▪

Chronicle Books   San Francisco

Copyright © 1991 by Nick Bantock. All rights reserved. No part of
this book may be reproduced in any form without written permission
from the publisher.

Printed in Hong Kong.
Book and cover design by Brenda Rae Eno.

ISBN: 0-87701-789-1

A note to the correspondent: these oversized postcards require the same
postage as a first-class letter.

Distributed in Canada by Raincoast Books,
112 East Third Avenue,
Vancouver, B.C., V5T 1C8

10 9 8 7 6 5 4 3 2 1

Chronicle Books
275 Fifth Street
San Francisco, California 94103

A Joke:

A woman walks into a butcher's shop and asks the butcher,
"Have you got a sheep's head?"
To which the butcher replies, "No, lady, that's just the way I part my hair."

Hearing this at the age of ten, I laughed till I cried. Thirty years later, I heard the same joke again, and I still laughed. Either I hadn't grown up, or it was highly durable (probably both). After a little pondering, I concluded that it was the sense-within-nonsense that gave it longevity. A few days later, I was glancing through my postcard collection when the idea of *The Missing Nose Flute* floated into my head. In captioning these cards, I've attempted to cross-pollinate my fondness for cliché with my illustrator's sense of the visually bizarre.

Carl and Sigy the teddy bears were my first postcard acquisition. I came across them in The Bristol Corn Exchange Flea Market. I couldn't believe that so much sexual innuendo could have gone so completely unrecognized. I stared, wondering if there were more monuments to innocence out there...and lo, there were hundreds.

—Nick Bantock

(Although the cards in this volume came from many different sources, I'd like to give special credit to the Weeda Stamp Store, which lets me rifle all the new old cards before anyone else gets their rotten hands on them.)

Ambidextrous though she was, retrieving her nose flute would be tricky.

To:

From *The Missing Nose Flute and Other Mysteries of Life*
copyright ©1991 by Nick Bantock, published by Chronicle Books.

In light of his destiny and the Clean Air Bill,
Young Winston was obliged to cut his habit to 40 a day.

To:

From *The Missing Nose Flute and Other Mysteries of Life*
copyright ©1991 by Nick Bantock, published by Chronicle Books.

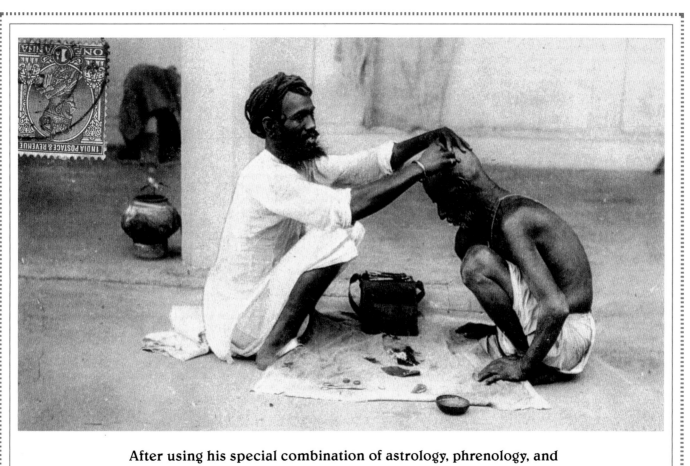

After using his special combination of astrology, phrenology, and
numerology, the seer portentously advised size 9 in green.

To:

From *The Missing Nose Flute and Other Mysteries of Life*
copyright © 1991 by Nick Bantock, published by Chronicle Books.

They could mock, but once he had the parts,
Maurice planned to install the nuclear warhead.

To:

From *The Missing Nose Flute and Other Mysteries of Life*
copyright ©1991 by Nick Bantock, published by Chronicle Books.

Mary had to understand, immaculate conception was in its infancy, and there were bound to be wrinkles.

To:

From *The Missing Nose Flute and Other Mysteries of Life*
copyright ©1991 by Nick Bantock, published by Chronicle Books.

The convent was not totally as Beatrice had envisioned it.

To:

From *The Missing Nose Flute and Other Mysteries of Life*
copyright ©1991 by Nick Bantock, published by Chronicle Books.

765 - Un jeu primitif.

"I AGREE, LAWRENCE, BUT WE HAVE TO FIT THE SAFEWAYS IN SOMEWHERE."

To:

From *The Missing Nose Flute and Other Mysteries of Life*
copyright ©1991 by Nick Bantock, published by Chronicle Books.

Watson knew Holmes was a master of disguise — but this was magnificent.

To:

From *The Missing Nose Flute and Other Mysteries of Life*
copyright ©1991 by Nick Bantock, published by Chronicle Books.

Mrs. John thought Elton might do better with glasses.

To:

From *The Missing Nose Flute and Other Mysteries of Life*
copyright ©1991 by Nick Bantock, published by Chronicle Books.

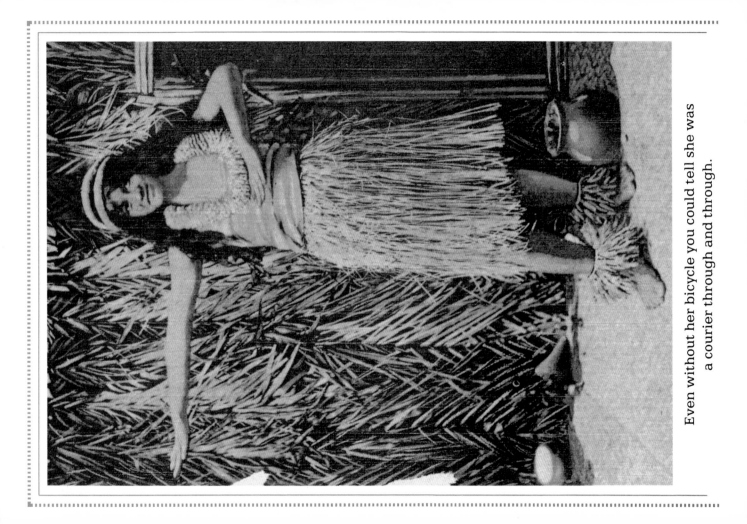

Even without her bicycle you could tell she was a courier through and through.

To:

From *The Missing Nose Flute and Other Mysteries of Life*
copyright ©1991 by Nick Bantock, published by Chronicle Books.

Instinctively, Gerald sensed that something was amiss with his stilts.

To:

From *The Missing Nose Flute and Other Mysteries of Life*
copyright ©1991 by Nick Bantock, published by Chronicle Books.

And at dusk, we'd sit back and air our souls.

To:

From *The Missing Nose Flute and Other Mysteries of Life*
copyright ©1991 by Nick Bantock, published by Chronicle Books.

She was the best quarterback he had ever dated.

To:

From *The Missing Nose Flute and Other Mysteries of Life*
copyright © 1991 by Nick Bantock, published by Chronicle Books.

"Why didn't the pretentious little twerp walk round the corner like any normal human being?" Arnold seethed.

To:

From *The Missing Nose Flute and Other Mysteries of Life*
copyright ©1991 by Nick Bantock, published by Chronicle Books.

A bright and happy Birthday!

Once again your birthday's here, dear
And I wish you every joy
Lots of cakes and all good things
For my Birthday boy.

Sigmund and Carl were always squabbling over the definition of sex.

To:

From *The Missing Nose Flute and Other Mysteries of Life*
copyright ©1991 by Nick Bantock, published by Chronicle Books.

He was beginning to feel the nurse wasn't taking his vasectomy as seriously as she ought.

To:

From *The Missing Nose Flute and Other Mysteries of Life*
copyright ©1991 by Nick Bantock, published by Chronicle Books.

The frankincense and myrrh would be a piece of cake, but getting the gold through customs was going to take some cover story.

To:

From *The Missing Nose Flute and Other Mysteries of Life*
copyright © 1991 by Nick Bantock, published by Chronicle Books.

Salut de l'Orient. Prière musulmane.

You never knew with Herb. He had so many unseen attachments.

To:

From *The Missing Nose Flute and Other Mysteries of Life*
copyright ©1991 by Nick Bantock, published by Chronicle Books.

Of all his toys Phyllis was the most aerodynamic.

To:

From *The Missing Nose Flute and Other Mysteries of Life*
copyright ©1991 by Nick Bantock, published by Chronicle Books.

Why was it, the twins mused, that as soon as a camera appeared, some politician wanted to pick you up and slobber all over you?

To:

From *The Missing Nose Flute and Other Mysteries of Life*
copyright ©1991 by Nick Bantock, published by Chronicle Books.

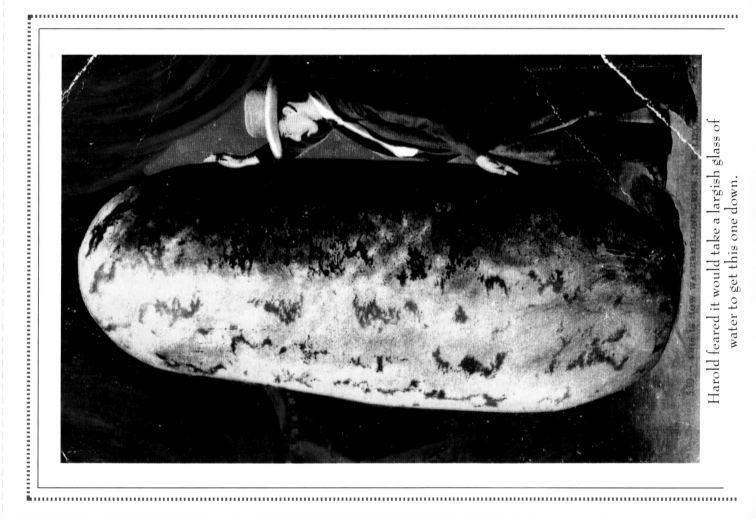

Harold feared it would take a largish glass of water to get this one down.

To:

From *The Missing Nose Flute and Other Mysteries of Life*
copyright © 1991 by Nick Bantock, published by Chronicle Books.

Putting Pinkerton and the failed suicide behind her,
Madame Butterfly took a job on the bootleg sake run.

To:

From *The Missing Nose Flute and Other Mysteries of Life*
copyright ©1991 by Nick Bantock, published by Chronicle Books.